Laugh Out Loud With 110 Parenting Quotes

By Kidsstoppress.com

Author's Note

"Making the decision to have a child is momentous. It is to decide forever to have your heart go walking around outside your body." If words could describe parenthood, these by Elizabeth Stone may just sum up the experience for many parents.

But there is another side to parenting - one that we share with you every morning at 9 AM on Instagram #kspmorninghumour so that you can begin your day with a smile. Don't get me wrong - parenting is a joy but raising kids is difficult and fraught with hurdles, rollercoasters, tears and peals of laughter.

I wanted to put this book together for those parents who just need a pick-me-up in between crazy days or want to know that other parents are struggling with the same craziness on some days.

Pick it up for a shot of inspiration (or comfort!) when you have 30 seconds in between changing nappies and feeding time. Or when you're busy asking questions to your teen, who rolls their eyes at you! As you flip through the pages, we guarantee you're going to go "Oh! This is so true!"

#simplifyingparenting

This makes for a great present for new parents, a quick read for current parents, or a coffee-table conversation starter.

We would love to know your favourite quotes from the book. Tag @kidsstoppress and @mansi.zaveri on Instagram

We hope you enjoy it as much as we have loved putting it together.

XOXO
Mansi Zaveri

#simplifyingparenting

Laugh Out Loud With 110 Parenting Quotes

By Kidsstoppress.com

1

Parenting is a lot like the bar scene:
Everyone's yelling, everything's sticky, it
is the same music over and over again and
occasionally someone pukes.

2

Woke up to my 6-year-old holding my hand this morning. It was such a sweet 3 seconds before I realised he was using my fingerprint to break into my phone.

3

80% of parenting is trying not to laugh when you're supposed to be mad.

4

Feeling guilty about the kids watching TV?
Just turn the captions on.
Boom!
Now they're reading.

5

I never realised how annoying I could be until
I created a miniature version of myself &
started to argue with it daily.

6

Whatever you do, do it with the confidence
of a 3-year-old in a Batman cape.

7

The funny thing about kids is that- they are the reason we lose it and the reason we hold it together.

8

Daughter: Mom, you're in my personal space.

Mom: You came out of my personal space.

9

You know you are a mom when- you have a messy bun all the time but want to dress your baby perfectly.

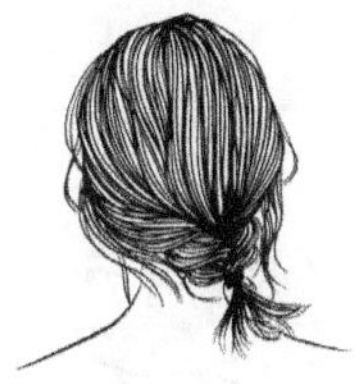

10

I just taught my kids how to make chai and now they're fighting over who gets to make it. My work here is done.

11

I heard that babies can recognise their mother's voice in the womb. Just so they can selectively block it out later.

12

The hardest stage of parenthood is whatever you're going through right now.

13

Every time I say, "No".
my kids hear. "Ask again, she didn't
understand the question."

14

The fastest land mammal is a toddler who's been asked what's in her mouth.

15

Parenthood is helping your child look for a toy you threw out three days ago.

#ksphu

mour

16

It doesn't matter how old your kids are, you'll always hear babies crying when you take a shower.

17

Sleeping with your child is like sharing a bed with a drunk octopus.

18

Right now, my kids are laughing and playing together beautifully. I like to call it, "pre-fighting".

19

Mothers be like: Need a break... But don't
trust a soul with their kids.
It's me.
I'm mothers.

20

Parenting is missing your kids when they are asleep, and missing your sanity when they are awake.

21

Trying to binge-watch a show when you are a parent takes 20 years, apparently.

22

Top 3 games moms play:
-What's that smell?
-What's that stain?
-What's that sound?

23

My parenting style is best described as ″No″ with a side of ″Ugh. Fine, but please don′t hurt yourself.″

24

I now know how it will end for me. One of my kids will unplug my life support to charge their iPad.

25

"I would describe my parenting style as gentle parenting with a sprinkle of sorry I lost my shit but y'all are driving me crazy."

26

Mom goal:
Being able to drink coffee hot.

27

I love how shocked my kids get when I lose my shit as if they didn't just spend the last 3 hours trying to make that happen.

28

Not to brag but my kids just listened to me the very seventh time I asked.

29

Husband: I'll watch the kids so
you can take a break.
Wife: Takes a break to fold the clothes and
empty the dishwasher.

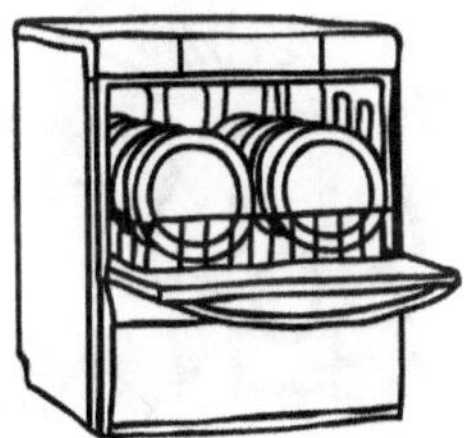

30

97% of parenting is just saying ″oh wow″ to your kid when they do something totally not wow.

31

"How was your vacation?"
"I didn't go on a vacation. I was babysitting my kids while they were on a vacation."

#parent

ingisfun

32

The book we really needed was
˝What to expect 17 years after you were
expecting...˝

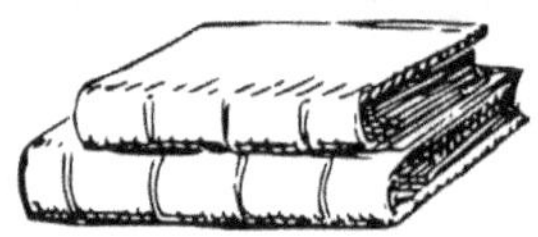

33

Welcome to the toddler years... you can leave your brain at the door.

34

Co-sleeping is where you clutch the edge of the mattress while your child acts like a board game spinner at the centre.

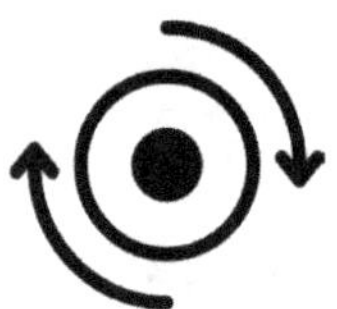

35

There are two types of children: those that get up in the middle of the night, and those who get up way too early.
And they are siblings.

36

My well-behaved firstborn gave me the
confidence to be a good mom.
My wild second kid taught me not to judge
other moms.

37

Babies are okay if you're into alarm clocks
that poop.

38

My son just showed me something he made and asked " Do you like it, or do you love it?" And those are the only options I'm giving people from now on.

39

My kids asked me what I used to play on the iPad when I was little, and I told them I used to speak into the fan to make me sound like a robot.

40

"MOTHERHOOD` is an extreme sport.
That's why we have to wear workout clothes
every day.

41

Nothing sexier than a man who wipes butts, blows noses and cooks dinner for his family.

42

If I could figure out a way to bottle my kids' energy and sell it to tired parents, I'd be a gazillionaire.

43

Being a mother taught me that catching vomit with my bare hands is better than cleaning it off the carpet.

44

Child: "Daddy's a lot nicer than you mommy."
Mom: "That's probably due to all the extra
rest he gets, sweetheart."

45

I have a question.
Does anyone know when kids start listening?
And by kids, I mean my mother-in-law's
kids. Specifically, her son. The one that I'm
married to.

46

I cried today at the thought of my
daughter leaving for college and getting
married and not living with me anymore...
Also, my daughter is 3.
Lol.

47

My daughter asked for a Cinderella-themed party.
So, I invited all of her friends over and made them clean my house.

#momli

febelike

I think my favourite part of being a mother has been sacrificing my body, career, mental stability and physical appearance to wait on them hand and foot.

Only to be met with, "You don't do anything for me" when I ask them to pick up a wrapper.

It's very rewarding.

49

Parenthood offers the unique experience of realising you are already late for something that doesn't start in the next four hours.

50

I wish I could clean as fast as my kids make a mess.

51

My trait is not letting anyone clean, because it's not clean unless I clean it. Then getting mad when no one helps me clean.

52

Having a teenager is like having a cat that only comes out to eat and hisses if you try to pet it.

53

By the age of 3, the average toddler has taken exactly 2 bites out of 327 bananas.

54

Parenting tip:
Only hike as far as you can carry your child.
I know this now.

#simplifyingparenting

55

My kids used to have a bedtime…
Now they just tuck me in and continue to do
whatever they want.

56

Silence is golden...
UNLESS you have kids.
Then silence is just suspicious.

57

A child: What's that?
Me holding an Oreo milkshake: It's spicy, you won't like it.

58

You know you're a mom to teenagers when
they text you a question while sitting right
next to you.

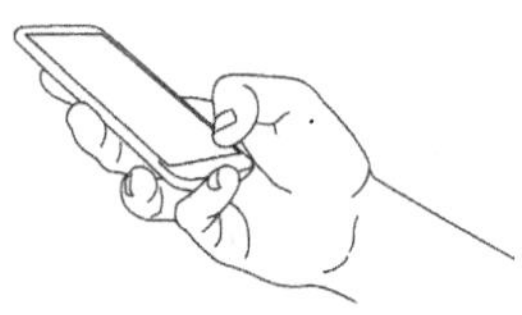

59

Me: I could use a good night's sleep.
My kids: We don't do that here.

60

Parenting is like folding a fitted sheet no one really knows how.

61

Reached the age when staying out past 10 is like a medical procedure.
I need a day to prep and a couple of days to recover.

62

How to calm a crying baby:
Pick up the baby.
Hold for approximately 5 years and gently
place back down.

63

I used the old "I gave birth to you" on my
daughter.
She said, "That was one time."

64

Motherhood is packing up everything for the beach and forgetting your own swimsuit.

65

Nothing's really lost...
Until mom can't find it.

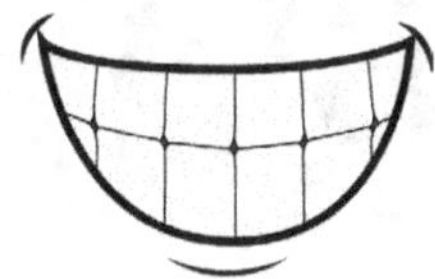

#laughterisgo

odforthesoul

66

"I'm tired from the whole entire day." -my
6yo at 9:13 am

67

Hey, parents of an only child considering having one more, know that I just split an M&M in half.
An M&M.
In half.

68

I'm just a mom standing in my teen's room looking for forks.

69

Pros and Cons of making kids:
Pros: Making.
Con: Kids.

70

If parenting came with a GPS, it would most probably say... Recalculating.

71

I didn't realise how much I loved sitting and doing nothing until I had kids and they wouldn't let me sit and do nothing.

72

Just a reminder that you're the parent and
you're in-charge.
Give that kid any colour cup you want!
LOL. I'm joking.
Don't do that- you'll die.

73

After my kids go to bed I just sit really still for
an hour and recover from the trauma.

74

"They're your kids too!"
My instructions to my husband when I leave
the house.

75

P.S. Your kindergarten teacher knows
EVERYTHING about you.
EVERYTHING.

76

I'm writing a book. It's called,
"I Wasn't Gonna Drink Tonight But..."
my children are my inspiration.

77

Having a child means whatever you did in your younger years will come back to haunt you.

#simplifyingparenting

78

Ready for another weekend of oversharing with a new mom and regretting it later.

79

I hate when I'm mad at my husband so I can't
show him a funny meme I'm looking at.

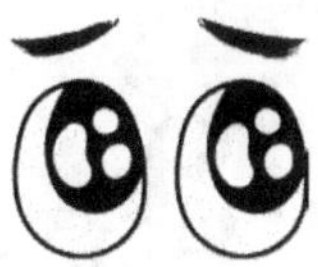

80

I wonder how long it's going to take for my kids to realise that I'm just winging it.

81

Nobody declines a call faster than a toddler
watching YouTube.

82

Me: I'm still young.
My bones: No, we're not.

83

Before becoming a parent, I had no idea how much time I'd spend secretly smuggling things into the trash.

#parenting

withhumour

84

I know my 6-year-old takes after me by how he sighs his way through all his homework.

85

I think I'm an easy-going parent until I watch my toddler eat an ice cream cone...

86

My friends asked me for suggestions for something short and dramatic to watch. So, I offered my 3-year-old son.

87

My son's superpower is to turn 1 cracker into 4.536 kgs of crumbs.

88

Parenting: Because sleep is unnecessary and who needs money?

89

No one prepares you for the transition from Ma-ma to Mommy to Mom to- Bruh!

90

I get more housework done in the
10 minutes before someone comes over than I
do in a week.

91

How to get your husband to fix something:
Act like you're about to fix it yourself.

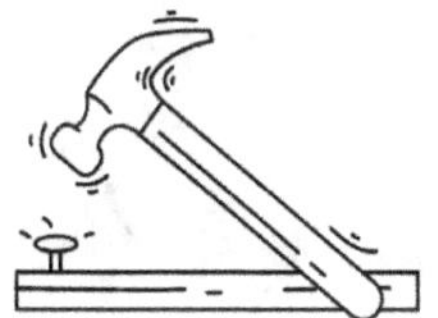

92

Currently approving my kids' friends based on which parents I think will drink wine with me on play dates.

93

Parenting gets easier when you learn to accept that kids are just all your worst qualities wrapped in the most beautiful packaging you've ever seen.

94

90% of parenting is convincing your child to participate in basic life necessities.
Eat, Sleep, Shower. Repeat.

95

Mary Poppins is my favourite movie
to watch because it's about a babysitter
coming from heaven to save parents from
watching their kids.

96

My daughter can never find her shoes, but she can find a microscopic piece of capsicum in her dinner.

Nothing humbles you faster than your toddler
complimenting your leg hair because they
look like daddy's.
Thanks, kid.

98

Before kids, I didn't understand the
expression "I can't hear myself think."
I get it now...

99

For a kid who says he hates loud noises, mine sure likes making them.

#simplifyingparenting

100

Parenting is just an endless cycle of wondering when a phase will end and then crying when a stage is over.

101

Being pregnant made me a side sleeper. Being a mom made me never sleep again.

102

Parenting hack:
There are no hacks.
Everything is hard.
These kids don't listen.
This is your life now.
Godspeed.

103

I think the hardest part of parenting my 7yo is pretending I'm even the slightest bit interested in Minecraft.

104

This can't be the same 9 pm I used to be starting to get ready for a night out at...

105

Sometimes, self-care looks like letting your kid go to bed in the princess dress that they wore all day because some things just aren't worth the meltdown.

106

The job description of a toddler is to trash the house and make washing. The job description of a parent is to tidy the house and do washing.

107

Can someone please tell me WHY my kids think it's a good time to talk to me when I'm blow-drying my hair?
It>s like they take the loudness as a challenge to be even louder.

108

I'm re-tired.
In the sense that I was tired yesterday.
And today, I am tired again.

109

I became a father the day my daughter was born, but I didn't become a dad until the first time she rolled her eyes at me.

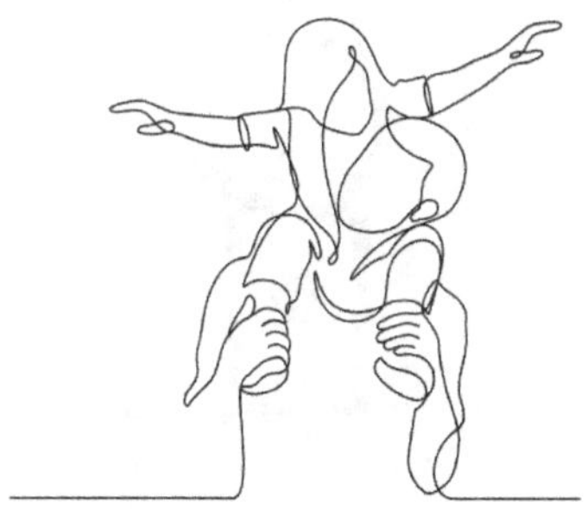

110

I shut my teen's room door every time the guests arrive, to make the house look cleaner.

#Thanks

@raisingteenstoday

@themomlifevlogs

@scarymommy

@katewouldhaveit

@hipmomma007

@mommydelight

@drinkingmommies

@sheridanholt

@momzilla.memes

Some of these quotes are inspired from fellow parents and most are from our real-life experiences.

We thank all parents for sharing their thoughts with the world.

#simplifyingparenting

While we wish our memories could keep track of all our memories could keep track of all our favourites, write down your favourite humour quotes so you can keep track of them all.

While we wish our memories could keep track of all our favourites, write down your favourite humour quotes so you can keep track of them all.

Team Credit

No one said parenting was easy. But that doesn't mean we can't have our share of fun and joy along the ride!

All of you have found our morning humour quotes so relatable. Most of you have asked us how do we always manage to get it right! The answer is 'coz we have been there, done that too! We have been in those shoes and know what you are dealing with at different points of the day and in different phases of your parenting life.

We would like to thank all those who have worked extremely hard to make the Parenting Quotes That Make You Laugh Out Loud book possible.

Mansi Zaveri for her drive, vision and passion. She's been the mentor we needed to drive this through. Without her unconditional support and constant encouragement this book would not have been possible.

Parul Gupta for being the steady anchor we always need for projects like this.. As a teen parent she needs a lot of laughter & tons of positive energy and through this book she's helped bring it to you too.

Tanya Lemos for her patience, the constant follow ups and for all the never ending changes we have been making to make this book perfect for you. Her calm and composure has been a great help in making sure this book delivered all that we promised.